World of Bugs
MYSTERIOUS MANTISES

By Greg Roza

Gareth Stevens
Publishing

Please visit our Web site, www.garethstevens.com. For a free color catalog of all our
high-quality books, call toll free 1-800-542-2595 or fax 1-877-542-2596.

Library of Congress Cataloging-in-Publication Data

Roza, Greg.
  Mysterious mantises / Greg Roza.
     p. cm. — (World of bugs)
   ISBN 978-1-4339-4604-2 (pbk.)
   ISBN 978-1-4339-4605-9 (6-pack)
   ISBN 978-1-4339-4603-5 (library binding)
   1. Praying mantis—Juvenile literature. I. Title.
   QL505.9.M35R69 2011
   595.7'27—dc22
                                        2010031814

First Edition

Published in 2011 by
Gareth Stevens Publishing
111 East 14th Street, Suite 349
New York, NY 10003

Editor: Greg Roza
Designer: Christopher Logan

Photo credits: Cover, pp. 1, 3, 5, 7, 9, 11, 13, 15, 17, 19, 21, 23 (all), 24 (all) Shutterstock.com.

Printed in the United States of America

CPSIA compliance information: Batch #CW11GS: For further information contact Gareth Stevens, New York, New York at 1-800-542-2595.

MYSTERIOUS MANTISES

A mantis has two big eyes.

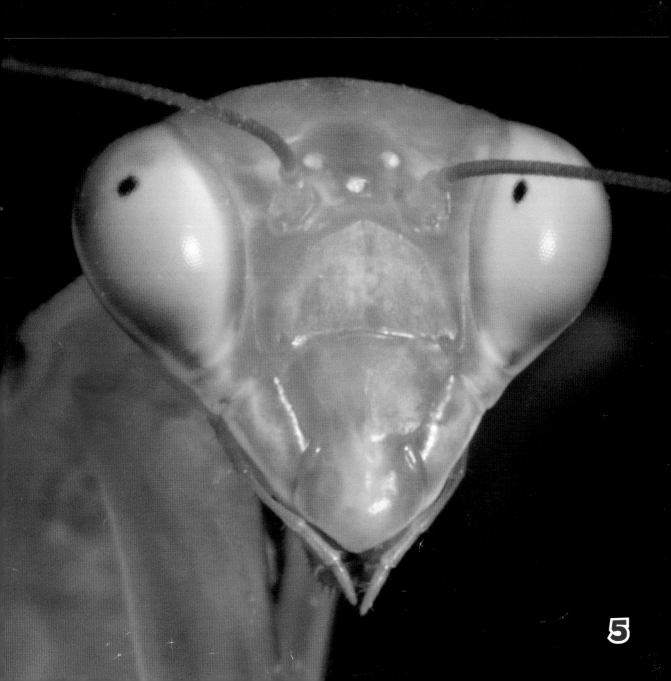

5

A mantis has two feelers.

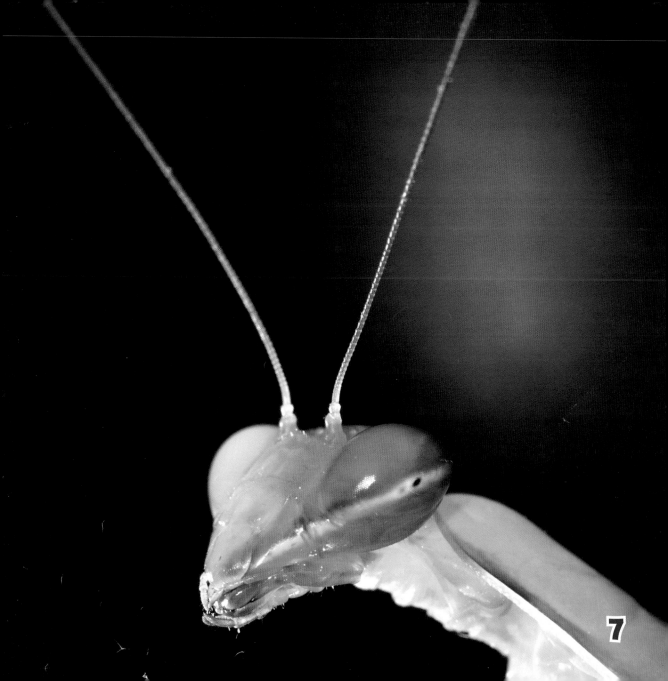

Most mantises have four wings.

A mantis has six legs.

A mantis uses its big front legs to catch food.

13

Most mantises eat bugs.

Mantises live in warm places.

17

This mantis is green.
A green mantis can
hide in leaves.

19

This mantis is brown.
A brown mantis can
hide in a tree.

21

Some mantises look
like flowers!

Words to Know

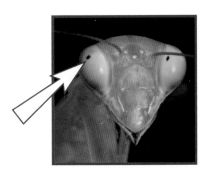

eye

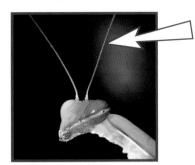

feeler

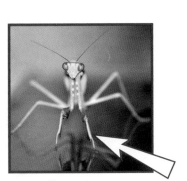

leg

wing

24